Frederic Remington

Sundown Leflare

Frederic Remington

Sundown Leflare

ISBN/EAN: 9783743360747

Manufactured in Europe, USA, Canada, Australia, Japa

Cover: Foto ©Thomas Meinert / pixelio.de

Manufactured and distributed by brebook publishing software (www.brebook.com)

Frederic Remington

Sundown Leflare

SUNDOWN
LEFLARE

Written and Illustrated by

FREDERIC REMINGTON

NEW YORK AND LONDON
HARPER & BROTHERS PUBLISHERS
1899

CONTENTS

ILLUSTRATIONS

THE GREAT MEDICINE-HORSE

AN INDIAN MYTH OF THE THUNDER

THE GREAT MEDICINE-HORSE

AN INDIAN MYTH OF THE THUNDER

"ITSONEORRATSEAHOOS," or Paint, as the white men called him, had the story, and had agreed to tell it to me. His tepee was not far, so "Sundown Leflare" said he would go down and interpret.

Sundown was cross-bred, red and white, so he never got mentally in sympathy with either strain of his progenitors. He knew about half as much concerning Indians as they did themselves, while his knowledge of white men was in the same proportion. I felt little confidence that I should get Paint's mysterious musings transferred to my head without an undue proportion of dregs filtered in from Sundown's lack of appreciation. While the latter had his special interest for me, the problem in this case was how to eliminate "Sundown" from "Paint." So much for interpreters.

We trudged on through the soft gray-blues of the moonlight, while drawing near to some tepees grouped in the creek bottom. The dogs came yelling; but a charge of Indian dogs always splits before an enemy which does not recoil, and recovers itself in their rear. There they may become dangerous. Sundown lifted the little tepee flap and I crawled through. A little fire of five or six split sticks burned brightly in the centre, illuminating old Paint as he lay back on his resting-mat. He

4

grunted, but did not move; he was smoking. We shook hands, and Sundown made our peace-offering to the squaw, who sat at her beading. We reclined upon the tepee and rolled cigarettes. There is a solemnity about the social intercourse of old Indian warriors which reminds me of a stroll through a winter forest. Every one knows by this how the interior of an Indian tepee looks, though every one cannot necessarily know how it feels; but most people who have wandered much have met with fleas. Talk came slow; but that is the Indian of it: they think more than they talk. Sundown explained something at length to Paint, and back came the heavy guttural clicking of the old warrior's words, accompanied by much subtle sign language.

"He sais he will tell you 'bout de horse. Now you got for keep still and wait ; he'll talk a heap, but you'll get de story eef you don' get oneasy."

" Now, Sundown, remember to tell me just what Paint says. I don't care what you think Paint means," I admonished.

" I step right in hees tracks."

Paint loaded his long red sandstone pipe with the utmost deliberation, sat up on his back-rest, and puffed with an exhaust like a small stationary engine. The squaw put two more sticks on the fire, which spitted and fluttered, lighting up the broad brown face of the old Indian, while it put a dot of light in his fierce little left eye. He spoke slowly, with clicking and harsh gutturals, as though he had an ounce of quicksilver in his mouth which he did not want to swallow. After a time Sundown raised his hand to enjoin silence.

" He sais dat God—not God, but dat

is bess word I know for white man ; I
have been school, and I know what he
want for say ces what you say medicin',
but dat ees not right. What he want
for say ees de ding what direct heem un
hees people what is best for do ; et ces
de speret what tell de old men who can
see best when dey sleep. Well—anyhow, it was long, long time ago, when
hees fader was young man, and 'twas
hees fader's fader what it all happened
to. The Absarokes deedn't have ponies 'nough—de horses ware new in de
country—dey used for get 'em out of a
lac,* 'way off somewhere — dey come
out of ee water, and dese Enjun† lay
in the bulrush for rope 'em, but dey
couldn't get 'nough ; besides de Enjun
from up north she use steal 'em from
Absaroke. Well — anyhow, de medicin' tole hees fader's fader dat he would

* Lake.   † Indian.

7

get plenty of horses eef he go 'way south. So small party went 'long wid heem—dey was on foot—dey was travel for long time, keep in de foothill. Dey was use for travel night un lay by daytime, 'cept when dey was hunt for de grub. De country was full up wid deir enemic, but de medicin' hit was strong, and de luck was weed 'em. De medicin' hit keep tellin' 'em for go 'long —go on—on—on—keep goin' long, long time. He's been tellin' me de names of revers dey cross, but you wouldn't know dem plass by what he call 'em. Dey keep spyin' camps, but the medicin' he keep tellin' 'em for go on, go on, un not bodder dem camp, un so dey keep goin'."

Here Sundown motioned Paint, and he started his strange, high-pitched voice — winking and moving his hands at Sundown, who was rolling a cigarette,

though keeping his eyes on the old
Indian. Presently the talking ceased.

"He sais—dey went on—what he is
tryin' for say ees dey went on so far hit
was heap hot, un de Enjun dey was
deeferent from what dees Enjun is.
He's tryin' for to get so far off dat I
don' know for tell you how far he ees."

"Never mind, Sundown; you stick to
Paint's story," I demanded.

"Well—anyhow—he's got dees outfit hell of a long way from home, un
dey met up wid a camp un heap of
pony. He was try tell how many pony
—like the buffalo use be—more pony
dan you see ober, by Gar. Den de
medicin' say dey was for tac dose pony
eef dey can. Well, den de outfit lay
roun' camp wid de wolf-skin on — de
white wolf. De Enjun he do jus' same
as wolf, un fool de oder Enjun, you see;
well, den come one night dey got de

9

herds whar dey wanted 'em, un cut out
all they could drive. Et was terrible
big bunch, 'cording as Paint say. Dey
drive 'em all night un all nex' day, wid
de horse-guides ahead, un de oders behin', floppin' de wolf-robe, un Paint say
de grass will nevar grow where dey pass
'long; but I dink, by Gar, Paint ees
talk t'ro' hees hat."

"Never mind—I don't want you to
think—you just freeze to old Paint's
talk, Mr. Sundown," I interlarded.

"Well, den—damn 'em, after dey had
spoil de grass for 'bout night un day de
people what dey had stole from come
a-runnin'. Et was hard for drive such
beeg bunch fas'—dey ought for have
tac whole outfit un put 'em foot; but
Paint say—un he's been horse-tief too
hisself, by Gar—he say dey natu'lly
couldn't; but I say—"

"Never mind what you say."

" Well, anyhow, I say—"

" Never mind, Sundown !"

" Well, ole Paint he say same t'ing.
" De oder fellers kim up wid 'em, so
just natu'lly dey went fightin' ; but dey
had extra horses, un de oder fellers dey
didn't, 'cep' what was fall out of bunch,
dem bein' slow horses, un horses what
was no 'count noway. Dey went runnin' un fightin' ' way in de night; but
de herd split on 'em, un he's fader's
fader went wid one bunch, un de oder
fellers went wid de 'split,' which no
one neber heard of no more. De men
what had loss de horses all went after
de oder bunch. Hees fader's fader
rode all dat night, all nex' day, un den
stopped for res'. Dar was only 'bout
ten men for look after de herd, which
was more horses dan you kin see een
dees valley to-day; what ees more horses
dan ten men kin wrangle, 'cordin' to me."

" Never mind, Sundown."

"Let 'er roll, Paint," said Leflare, beginning a new cigarette.

"He sais," interrupted Sundown, "dey was go 'long slow, slow — goin' towards de village—when one day dey was jump by dose Cheyenne. Dey went runnin' an' fightin' till come night, un couldn't drive de herd rightly. Dey loss heap of horses, but as dey come onto divide, dey saw camp right in front of dem. It was 'mos' night, so four or five of hees fader's fader's men dey cut out a beeg bunch, and spilt hit off down a coulie. De Enjun foller de oder bunch, which ram right eento de village, whar the 'hole outfit went for fight lac * hell. Paint's fader's fader she saw dees as she rode ober de hill. Dey was loss heap of men dat day by bein' kill un by run eento dose camp—lese-

* Like.

wise none of dem ever show up no more. Well, den, Paint say dey was keep travellin' on up dees way—hit was tac heem d—— long story for geet hees fader's fader's outfit back here, wheech ces hall right, seein' he got 'em so far 'way for begin wid."

Then Paint continued his story:

"He sais de Sioux struck 'em one day, un dey was have hell of a fight—runnin' deir pony, shootin' deir arrow. One man he was try mount fresh horse, she stan' steel un buck, buck, buck, un dees man he was not able for geet on; de Sioux dey come run, run, un dey kiell* heem. You see, when one man he catch fresh horse, he alway' stab hees played-out horse, 'cause he do not want eet for fall eento hand of de Enjun follerin'. Den White Bull's horse she run slow; he 'quirt' heem, but eet was do

* Kill.

no good—ze horse was done; de Sioux dey was shoot de horse, un no one know whatever becom' of heem, but I dink he was kiell all right 'nough. Den 'noder man's horse she was stick hees foot in dog-hole, un de Sioux dey shoot las' man 'cept hees fader's fader. Den he was notice a beeg red horse what had alway' led de horse ban' since dey was stole. Dese Enjun had try for rope dees horse plenty times, but dey was never been able, but hees fader's fader was ride up to de head of de ban', un jus' happen for rope de red horse. He jump from hees pony to dees red horse jus' as Sioux was 'bout to run heem down. De big red horse was run—run run lac hell — ah! He was run, by Gar, un de Sioux dey was—aah!—de Sioux dey couldn't run wid de big red horse nohow.

"He was gone now half-year, un he

"HE JUMP FROM HEES PONY TO DEES RED HORSE"

deed not know where he find hees people. He was see coyote runnin' 'head,
un he was say 'good medicin'.' He
foller after leetle wolf—he was find two
buffalo what was kiell by lightnin', what
show coyote was good medicin'. He
was give coyote some meat, un nex' day
he was run on some Absaroke, who was
tell him whar hees people was, wheech
was show how good de coyote was.
When he got camp de Enjun was terrible broke up, un dey had nevar before
see red horse. All of deir horses was
black, gray, spotted, roan, but none of
dem was red—so dees horse was tac to
de big medicin' in de medicin'-lodge,
un he was paint up. He got be strong
wid Absaroke, un hees fader's fader was
loss horse because he was keep in medicin'-tepee, un look after by big medicin'-
chiefs. Dey was give out eef he was
loss eet would be bad, bad for Absa-

roke, un dey was watch out mighty close
—by Gar, dey was watch all time dees
red horse. When he go out for graze,
t'ree warriors was hole hees rope un
t'ree was sit on deir pony 'longside. No
one was ride heem."

Then, talking alternately, the story
came: "He sais de horse of de Absaroke was increase—plenty pony—un de
mare he was all red colts; de big horse
was strong. De buffalo dey was come
right to de camp—by Gar, de horse was
good. De Sioux sent Peace Commis-
sion for try buy de horse—dey was do
beesness for Enjun down whar de summer come from, what want for geet heem
back—for he was a medicin'-horse. De
Absaroke dey was not sell heem. Den
a big band of de Ogalalas, Brulés, Min-
neconjous, Sans Arcs, Cheyennes, was
come for tac de red horse, dey was kiell
one village, but dare was one man 'scape,

what was come to red horse, un de Absaroke dey was put de red paint on deir
forehead. Ah! de Sioux dey was not
get de red horse — dey was haf to go
'way. Den some time de beeg medicin'-horse was have hell of a trouble wid
de bigges' medicin'-chief, right in de big
medicin - lodge. Dees word medicin'
don't mean what de Enjun mean ; de
tent whar de sperets come for tell de
people what for do, ees what dey mean ;
all same as Fader Lacomb he prance
'roun' when he not speak de French—
dat's what dey mean. All right, he
have dees trouble wid de head chief, un
he keek heem cen de head, un he kiell
him dead. After dat he was get for be
head medicin'-chief hisself, un he tole
all de oder medicin' - chief what for do.
He was once run 'way from de men
what was hol' hees rope when he was
graze — dey was scared out of deir

life of heem eef dey was mak' heem
mad, un he was go out een herd un
kiell some horse. No one was dare go
after heem. De medicin'-men dey was
go out wid de big medicin' — dey was
talk come back to heem; but he
wouldn't come. Den de virgin woman
of de tribe — she was kind of medicin'-
man herself — she was go out un make
a talk; she was tell red horse to go off
—dat's de way for talk to people when
deir minds not lac oder people's minds
—un de horse she was let heem bring
heem back. After dat all de Absaroke
women had for behave preety well, or
de medicin'-men kiell dem, 'cause dey
say de medicin'-horse she was want de
woman for be better in de tribe. Be
d—— good t'ing eef dat horse she 'roun'
here now."

"Oh, you reptile! will you never mind
this thinking—it is fatal!" I sighed.

THE MYSTERY OF THE THUNDER

"Well, anyhow, he sais de woman
dey was have many pappoose, un de
colts was red, un was not curly hair, un
de 'yellow eyes'* was come wid de
gun for trade skin. De buffalo she was
stay late; de winter was mile; de enemy no steal de pony, un de Absaroke
he tac heap scalp — all dese was medicin'-horse work. But in de moon een
which de geese lay deir eggs de great
horse he was rise up een de curl of de
smoke of de big lodge—he was go plum'
t'ro de smoke-hole. De chief ask him
for not go, but he was say he was go
to fight de T'under-Bird. He say he
would come back. Dey could keep his
ghost. So he went 'way, un since den
he has nevar come back no more. But
Paint say lots of ole men use for see
heem go t'ro' air wid de lightnin' comin'
out of his nose, de T'under-Bird al-

* White men.

ways runnin' out of hees way; he was
always lick de t'under. Paint say dese
Enjun have not yet see de medicin'-
horse nowday; eef dey was seen heem
more, dey see no 'yellow eyes' een
dees country. He sais he has seen de
medicin' - horse once. He was hunt
over een de mountain, but he was not
have no luck; he was hungry, un was
lay down by leetle fire een cañon. He
was see de beeg medicin'-horse go 'long
de ridge of de hill 'gainst de moon—he
was beeg lac de new school - house.
Paint got up un talked loud to de
horse, askin' heem eef he was nevar
come back. De horse stop un sais—
muffled, lac man talk t'ro' blanket—
Yes, he was come back from speret-
land, when he was bring de buffalo
plenty; was roll de lan' over de white
men; was fight de north wind. He
sais he was come back when de Absa-

THE GOING OF THE MEDICINE-HORSE

roke was not wear pants, was ride wid-
out de saddle ; when de women was on
de square—un, by Gar, I t'ink he not
come varric soon."

" What does Paint say ?"

" Ah, Paint he sais hit weel all come
some day."

" Is that all ?"

" Yes—dat ees all," said Sundown.

To be sure, there is quite as much
Sundown in this as Paint—but if you
would have more Paint, it will be neces-
sary to acquire the Crow language, and
then you might not find Paint's story
just as I have told it.

HOW ORDER NO. 6 WENT THROUGH

AS TOLD BY SUNDOWN LEFLARE

HOW ORDER NO. 6 WENT THROUGH

AS TOLD BY SUNDOWN LEFLARE

WE were full of venison and coffee
as we gathered close around the camp-
fire, wiping the fitful smoke out of our
eyes alternately as it came our way.

" It's blowing like the devil," said the
sportsman, as he turned up his face to
the pine-trees.

" Yees, sair. Maybeso dar be grass
fire secon' ting we know," coincided
Sundown Leflare.

Silver - Tip, the one who drove the
wagon, stood with his back to us, gaz-

ing out across the mountain to an ominous red glare far to the south. "Ef that forest fire gets into Black Canyon, we'll be straddlin' out of yer all sorts of gaits before mornin'," he remarked.

"Cole night," observed Bear-Claw, which having exhausted his stock of English, he spoke further to Fire-Bear, but his conversation was opaque to us.

"Look at the stars!" continued the sportsman.

"Yes—pore critters—they have got to stay out all night; but I am going to turn in. It's dam cold," and Silver-Tip patted and mauled at his blankets.

"What was the coldest night you ever saw?" I asked.

He pulled off his boots, saying: "Seen heap of cold nights—dun'no' what was the coldest — reckon I put in one over on the Bull Mountains, winter of '80, that I ain't going to forget. If nex' day hadn't been a Chinook, reckon I'd be thar now."

"You have been nearly frozen, I suppose, Sundown?" I added.

"Yees, sair — I was cole once all right."

"Ah—the old coffee-cooler, he's been cold plenty of times. Any man what lives in a tepee has been cold, I reckon; they've been that way six months for a stretch," and having made this good-natured contribution, Silver-Tip pulled his blanket over his head.

Sundown's French nervousness rose. "Ah—dat mule-skinner, what she know 'bout cole? — she freeze on de green grass. I freeze seex day in de middle of de wintar over dar Buford. By gar, dat weare freeze too! Come dam near put my light out. Um-m-m!" and I knew that Sundown was my prey.

"How was that?"

" Over Fort Keough — I was scout
for Ewers — she was chief scout for
Miles," went on Leflarc.

"Yas, I was scout too—over Keough
—same time," put in Ramon, the club-
footed Mexican.

" Yees, Ramon was scout too. Say—
Miles she beeg man Eas'—hey ? I see
her come troo agency—well, fall of '90.
Ah, she ole man ; don' look like she use
be sebenty-seben. Good-lookin' den."

" Wall—what you spect?" sighed his
congener Ramon, in a harsh interrup-
tion. " I was good-lookin' mon myself
—sebenty-seben."

" You weare buy more squaw dan you
weare eber steal — you ole frog. Dat
Miles she was mak heap of trouble up
dees way. I was geet sebenty dollar a
month. She not trouble my people,
but she was no good for Cheyenne un
Sioux. Dey was nevar have one good

night sleep af'er she was buil' de log house on de Tongue Rivière. Ah, ha, we was have hell of a time dem day'— don' we, Wolf-Voice?" and that worthy threw up his head quickly, and said, "Umph!"

"Well—I was wid my ole woman set in de lodge one day. Eet was cole. Lieutent Ewers she send for me. I was know I was got for tak eet or lose de sebenty. Well, I tak eet. Eet was cole.

"I was tink since, it weare dam good ting I lose dat sebenty. I was geet two pony, un was go to log house, where de officier she write all time in de book. Lieutent was say I go to Buford. I was say eet dam cole weddar for Buford. Lieutent was say I dam coffee-cooler. Well—I was not. Sitts-on-the-Point and Dick, she white man, was order go Buford wid me. Lieutent was say, when she han' me beeg lettair wid de red button, 'You keep eet clean, Leflare, un you go troo.' I tole heem I was go troo, eef eet was freeze de steamboat.

"We was go out of de fort on our pony—wid de led horse. We was tak' nothin' to eat, 'cause we was eat de buffalo. I was look lak de leetle buffalo—all skin. Skin hat—skin robe— skin leggin—you shoot me eef you see me. Eet was cole. We weare ride lak hell. When we was geet to Big Dry, Dick she say, 'Your pony no good; your pony not have de oat; you go back.' He says he mak Buford to-morrow night. I say, 'Yees, we go back to-morrow.'

"We mak leetle sleep, un Sitts-on-the-Point he go back Keough, but I geets crazy, un say I brave man; I weel not go back; I weel go Buford, or give de dinner to de dam coyote. I weel go.

"My pony he was not able for run, un Dick she go over de heel—I was see her no more. I was watch out for de buffalo—all day was watch. I was hungry; dar was nothin' een me. All right, I was go top of de heel — I was not see a buffalo. All dese while I was head for de Mountain - Sheep Buttes, where I know Gros Ventre camp up by Buford. Eet was blow de snow, un I was walk heap for keep warm. I was tink, eef no buffalo, no Gros Ventre camp for Leflare, by gar. I was marry Gros Ventre woman once, un eef I was geet dar I be all right. De snow she blow, un I could see not a ting. When eet geet dark, I was not know where I was go, un was lay down een de willow bush. Oh, de cole — how de hell you spect I sleep? — not sleep one wink, 'cept one. Well, my pony was try break away, but I was watch 'im, 'cept dat one wink. De dam pony what was led horse, she was geet off een de one wink. I see her track een de mornin', but I was not able for run him wid de order pony. He was geet clean away. 'Bout dat I was sorry, for een de day-time I was go keel heem eef no buffalo.

"Een de mornin' de win' she blow; de snow she blow too. Eet was long time 'fore I untie my lariat, un couldn't geet on pony 'tall—all steef—all froze. I walk long—walk long;" and Sundown shrugged up his shoulders and eyebrows, while he shut down his eyes and mouth in a most forlorn way. He had the quick, nervous French delivery of his father, coupled with the harsh voice of his Indian mother. There was also much of the English language employed by this waif of the plains which, I know, you will forgive me if I do not introduce.

" I deedn't know where I was—I was los'—couldn't see one ting. Was keep under cut bank for dodge win'. De snow she bank up een plass, mak me geet out on de pararie, den de win' she mak me hump. Pony he was heavy leg for punch troo de snow. All time I was watch out for buffalo, but dar was no buffalo ;" and Sundown's voice rose in sympathy with the frightful condition which haunted his memory.

" Begin tink my medicin' was go plumb back on me. Den I tink Ewers —wish she out here wid dam ole order. Eet mak me mad. Order — all time order — by gar, order soldier to change hees shirt — scout go two hundred miles. My belly she draw up like tomtom, un my head go roun', roun',

lak ting Ramon was mak de hair rope
wid; my han' she shake lak de leaf
de plum - tree. I was fall down under
cut bank, wid pony rope tie roun' me.
Pony he stay, or tak me wid heem.
How long I lay—well, I dun'no', but I
was cole un wak up. Eet was steel—de
star she shine; de win' she stop blow.
Long time I was geet up slow. I was
move leetle — move leetle—deen I was
move queek—move leetle—move queek.
All right—you eat ten deer reebs while
I was geet up un stan' on my feet. Pony
he was white wid de snow un de fros'.
Buffalo-robe she steef lak de wagon box.
Long time I was move my finger—was
try mak fire, un after while she blaze
up. Ah, good fire — she steek in my
head. Me un pony we geet thaw out
one side, den oder side. I was look at
pony—pony was look at me. By gar—
I tink he was 'fraid I eat heem; but I

"'UN I WAS YELL TERRIBLE'"

was say no—I eat him by-un-by. I was melt de snow een my tin cup — was drink de hot water—eet mak me strong. Den come light I was ride to beeg butte, look all roun' — all over, but couldn't tell where I was. Den I was say, no buffalo I go Missouri Rivière.

"Long time, I was come to de buffa-lo. Dey was all roun'—oh, everywhere—well, hundred yard. When I was geet up close, I was aim de gun for shoot. I couldn't hole dat gun — she was wabble lak de pony tail een de fly-time. All right, I shoot un shoot at de dam buffalo, but I neber heet eem 'tall—all run off. My head she swim ; my han' she shake ; my belly she come up een my neck un go roun' lak she come untie. I almos' cry.

"Well—I dun'no' jus' what den. 'Pears lak my head she go plumb off. I was wave my gun ; was say I not afraid of de Sioux. Dam de Sioux! —I was fight all de Sioux in de worl'. I was go over de snow fight dem, un I was yell terrible. Ect seem lak all de Sioux, all de Cheyenne, all de Assiniboine, all de bad Enjun een de worl', she come out of de sky, all run dar pony un wave dar gun. I could hear dar pony gallop ovar my head. I was fight 'em all, but dey went 'way.

"A girl what I was use know she come drop—drop out of de sky. She had kettle of boil meat, but she was not come right up—was keep off jus' front of my pony. I was run after de girl, but she was float 'long front of me—I could not catch her. Den I don' know nothin'.

"Black George un Flyin' Medicin' was two scout come to Keough from Fort Peck. Dey saw me un follow me —dey was go to keel me, but dey see I was Leflare, so dey rope my pony, tak me een brush, mak fire, un give me leetle meat. By come night I was feel good—was geet strong.

"We was 'fraid of de Assiniboine—'cause de order fellers had seen beeg sign. I sais let us go 'way mile or so un leave fire burn here.

"Black George he sais he no dam ole woman—he brav man—fight dem—no care dam for Assiniboine.

"I say to myself, all right — Assiniboine been foller you. I go.

"Flyin' Medicin' he want for go, but George he sais Assiniboine scare woman wid hees pony track — umph! un Flyin' Medicin' she sais she no ole woman. I say, by gar, I am woman ; I have got sense. You wan' stay here you be dead. Den I tak my pony un I go 'way een de dark, but I look back dar un see Medicin', she lie on de robe,

Black George she set smoke de pipe,
un a gray dog he set on de order side,
all een de firelight. I sais dam fools.

"Well, I got for tell what happen.
When I was go 'bout mile I was lay
down. 'Bout one hour I hear hell of
shootin'. I geet up queek, climb pony,
run lak hell. I was ole woman, un I
was dam glad for be ole woman. Eet
was dark; pony was very thin; all same
I make heap of trail 'fore mornin' bes'
I could."

I asked Sundown what made the
shooting.

"Oh—Black George camp—course I
deedn't know, but I was tink strong eet
bee hees camp all right 'nough. Long
time after I hear how 'twas. Well—
dey lay dar by de fire — Medicin' on
hees back—George she set up—dog he
set up order side—Assiniboine come on
dar trail. I was ole woman—eef not,

"SHE WAS KEEP OFF JUS' FRONT OF MY PONY".

maybeso I was set by de fire too—
humph !

"George he geet no chance fight
Assiniboine. Dey fire on hees camp,
shoot Flyin' Medicin' five time — all
troo chest, all troo leg, all troo neck—
all shoot up. Black George she was
shot t'ree time troo lef' arm ; un, by
gar, gray dog she keel too. Black
George grab hees gun un was run jump
down de cut bank. Assiniboine was
rush de camp un run off de pony, but
George she was manage wid her lef'
han' to shoot over cut bank, un dey
was not dare tak Medicin's hair. Black
George he was brave man. He was talk
beeg, but he was as beeg as hees talk.
He was scout roun', un was see no Assiniboine ; he was come to Flyin' Medicin', who was go gurgle, gurgle—oh, he
was all shot — all blood " — and here
Sundown made a noise which was aw-

fully realistic and quite unprintable, showing clearly that he had seen men who were past all surgery.

"George she raise Medicin' up, was res' hees head on hees arm, un den Medicin' was give heem hell. He was say: 'Deedn't I tole you? By gar, you dam brave man; you dam beeg fool! You do as I tole you, we be 'live, by gar. Now our time has come.' When he could speak again—when he had speet out de blood—he sais, 'Go geet my war-bag—geet out my war-bonnet—my bead shirt—my bead moccasins—put 'em on me—my time has come'; un Black George she geet out all de fine war-clothes, un she dress Medicin' up—all up een de war-clothes. 'Put my medicin'-bag on my breas'—good-bye, Black George, keek de fire—good-bye'; un Medicin' die all right.

" Course Black George she put out a foot un mak trail for Keough. He was haf awful time ; was seex day geet to buffalo - hunter camp, where she was crawl mos' of de way. De hunter was geeve heem de grub, un was pull heem to Keough een dar wagon. Reckon he was cole — all de blood run out hees arm—nothin' to eat—seex day—reckon dat ole mule - skinner she tink she was cole eef she Black George."

" What became of you meanwhile ?"

" Me? Well — I was not stop until come bright day ; den my pony was go deese way, was go dat way "—here Sundown spread out his finger-tips on the ground and imitated the staggering forefeet of a horse.

" I was res' my pony half day, un was try keel buffalo, but I was weak lak leetle baby. My belly was draw up — was go roun' — was turn upside-down—was hurt me lak I had wile-cat inside my reebs. De buffalo was roun' dar. One minute I see 'em all right, nex' minute dey go roun' lak dey was all drunk. No use — I could not keel buffalo. Eet was Gros Ventre camp or bus' Leflare wid me den. All time eet very cole; fros' go pop, pop under pony feet. Guess I look lak dead man— guess I feel dam sight worse. Dat seex day she mak me very ole man.

"I was haf go slow—pony he near done—jus' walk 'long. I deedn't care dam for Assiniboine now. De gray wolf he was follow 'long behin'—two— t'ree — four wolf. I deedn't care dam for wolf. All Sioux, all Assiniboine, all wolf een de worl'—she go to hell now; I no care. I was want geet to Gros Ventre camp 'fore I die. I was walk 'long slow — was feed my pony; my feet, my han's was get cold, hard lak

knife-blade. I was haf go to cut bank
for fall on my pony's back—no crawl
up no more. I was ride all night, slow,
slow. Was sit down; wolf was come up
look at me. I was tell wolf to go to
hell.

"Nex' day same ting—go 'long slow.
Pony he was dead; he no care for me.
I can no more keek heem; I cannot use
whip; I was dead.

"You ask me eef I was ever froze—
hey, what you tink? Dat mule-skinner,
Silver-Tip, he been dar—by gar, he
nevair melt all nex' summer.

"Jus' dark I was come een big timber by creek. I was tink I die dar, for
I could not mak de fire. I was stan'
steel lak de steer een de coulee when
de blizzair she blow. Den what you
tink? I was hear Gros Ventre woman
talk 'cross de rivière. She was come
geet de wattair. I was lead de pony

43

on de hice. I was not know much, but I was wake up by fall een wattair troo crack een hice. My rein was 'roun' my shoulder; my gun she cross my two arm. I could not use my han'. When I was fall, gun she catch 'cross hice— pony was pull lak hell — was pull me out. I was wet, but I was wake up. Eef dat bridle she break, een de spring-time dey fine Leflare een wheat - fiel' down Dakotah.

"De woman was say, 'Go below— you find de ford.' Den he was run. After while I get 'cross ford — all hice. Was come dam near die standin' up. I was see leetle log house, un was go to door un pound wid my elbow. 'Let me een—let me een—I froze,' sais I, een Gros Ventre.

" Dey say, ' Who you are ?'

"I sais, ' I am Leflare — I die een 'bout one minute—let me een.'

" ' You talk Gros Ventre ; maybeso you bad Engun. How we know you Leflare ?' sais de woman.

" ' Eef I not Leflare, shoot when you open de door,' un dey open de door. I tink dey was come near shoot me — I was look terrible — dey was 'fraid. I grab de fire, but dey was pull me 'way. Dey was sit on me un tak off my clothes un rub me wid de snow. Well, dey was good ; I dun'no' what dey do, but I was eat, eat, leetle at a time, till I was fall 'sleep. When I was wake up I was say, ' Tak dam ole order to Buford,' un I was tole de man what was tak eet I was keel heem eef he not tak eet.

" I lay een dat log house t'ree day 'fore I geet out, un den I go Buford. Dey sais de order she was all right. Den dey want me go back Keough wid order. I sais, ' Dam glad go back,' for

45

de weddar she was fine den. 'You geeve me pony.'

"'Why geeve you pony?' sais de officier.

"'By gar, de las' order she keel my pony,' I sais."

SUNDOWN LEFLARE'S
WARM SPOT

SUNDOWN LEFLARE'S
WARM SPOT

TOWARDS mid - day the steady brilliancy of the sun had satiated my color sense, and the dust kicked up in an irritating way, while the chug-a-chug, chug-a-chug of the ponies began to bore me. I wished for something to happen.

We had picked wild plums, which had subdued my six-hour appetite, but the unremitting walk-along of our march had gotten on my nerves. A proper man should not have such fussy things—but I have them, more is the pity. The pony was going beautifully: I could not

D   49

quarrel with him. The high plains do things in such a set way, so far as weather is concerned, and it is a day's march before you change views. I began to long for a few rocks — a few rails and some ragged trees — a pool of water with some reflections — in short, anything but the horizontal monotony of our surroundings.

To add to this complaining, it could not be expected that these wild men would ever stop until they got there, wherever "there" might happen to be this day. I evidently do not have their purpose, which is "big game," close to my heart. The chickens in this creek-bottom which we are following up would suit me as well.

These people will not be diverted, though I must, so I set my self-considering eye on Sundown Leflare. He will answer, for he is a strange man,

with his curious English and his weird
past. He is a tall person of great phys-
ical power, and must in his youth have
been a handsome vagabond. Born and
raised with the buffalo Indians, still
there was white man enough about him
for a point of view which I could understand. His great head, almost Roman,
was not Indian, for it was too fine; nor
was it French; it answered to none of
those requirements. His character was
so fine a balance between the two, when
one considered his environment, that I
never was at a loss to place the inflec-
tions. And yet he was an exotic, and
could never bore a man who had read
a little history.

Sombreroed and moccasined, Sundown pattered along on his roan pinto,
talking seven languages at the pack-
ponies, and I drew alongside. I knew he
never contributed to the sum of human

knowledge gratuitously ; it had to be ir-
ritated out of him with delicacy. I won-
dered if he ever had a romance. I knew
if he ever had, it would be curious. We
bumped along for a time doggedly, and
I said,

" Where you living now, Sundown ?"

Instantly came the reply, " Leevin'
here." He yelled at a pack-horse ; but
turning with a benignant smile, added,
" Well, I weare leeve on dees pony, er
een de blanket on de white pack-horse."

" No tepee ?" I asked.

" No — no tepee," came rather sol-
emnly for Sundown, who was not sol-
emn by nature, having rather too much
variety for that.

" I suppose you are a married man ?"

" No—no—me not marry," came the
heavy response.

" Had no woman, hey?" I said, as I
gave up the subject.

"Oh, yees! woman—had secx woman," came the rather overwhelming information.

"Children too, I suppose?"

"Oh, dam, yes! whole tribe. Why, I was have boy old as you aire. He up Canada way; hees mudder he Blackfoot woman. Dat was 'way, 'way back yondair, when I was firs' come Rocky Mountain. I weare a boy."

I asked where the woman was now.

"Dead—long, long time. She got keel by buffalo. She was try for skin buffalo what was not dead 'nough for skin. Buffalo was skin her," and Sundown grinned quickly at his pleasantry; but it somehow did not appeal to my humor so much as to my imagination, and it revealed an undomesticated mind.

"Did you never have one woman whom you loved more than all the others?" I went on.

53

"Yees; twenty year 'go I had Gros
Ventre woman. She was fine woman—
bes' woman I evair have. I pay twenty-five pony for her. She was dress de
robe un paint eet bettair, un I was mak
heap of money on her. But she was
keel by de Sioux while she was one day
pick de wil' plum, un I lose de twenty-
five pony een leetle ovair a year I have
her. Sacré !

"Eef man was hab seex woman lak
dat een dose day, he was not ask de
odds of any reech man. He could sell
de robe plenty;" and Sundown heaved
a downright sigh.

I charged him with being an old trader, who always bought his women and
his horses; and Sundown turned his
head to me with the chin raised, while
there was the wild animal in his eye.

"Buy my woman! What de 'ell you
know I buy my woman ?"

And then I could see my fine work. I gave him a contemptuous laugh.

Then his voice came high-pitched: "You ask me de oddar night eef I weare evair cole. Do you tink I was evair cole now? You say I buy my woman. Now I weel tell you I deed not alway buy my woman."

And I knew that he would soon vindicate his gallantry, so I said, softly, " I will have to believe what you tell me about it."

" I don' wan' for dat agent to know 'bout all dees woman beesness. He was good frien' of mine, but he pretty good man back Eas' — maybeso he not lak me eef he know more 'bout me ;" and Sundown regained his composure.

" Oh, don't you fret — I won't say a word," I assured him. And here I find myself violating his confidence in print ;

but it won't matter. Neither Sundown nor the agent will ever read it.

"'Way back yondair, maybeso you 'bout dees high"—and he leaned down from his pony, spreading his palm about two feet and a half above the buffalo-grass—" I was work for Meestar Mac-Donnail, what hab trade-pos' on Missouri Reever. I was go out to de Enjun camp, un was try for mak 'em come to Meestar MacDonnail for trade skin. Well, all right. I was play de card for dose Enjun, un was manage for geet some skin myself for trade Meestar MacDonnail. I was know dose Enjun varrie well. I was play de card, was run de buffalo, un was trap de skin.

" I was all same Enjun—fringe, bead, long hair—but I was wear de hat. I was hab de bes' pony een de country, un I was hab de firs' breech-loadair een de country. Ah, I was reech! Well, I

young man, un de squaw she was good frien' for me, but Snow-Owl hab young woman, un he tink terrible lot 'bout her —was watch her all time. Out of de side of her eye she was watch me, un I was watch her out of de side of my eye —we was both watch each oddar, but we deed not speak. She was look fine, by gar! You see no woman at Billings Fair what would spect even wid her. I tink she not straight-bred Enjun woman—I tink she 'bout much Enjun as I be. All time we watch each oddar. I know eet no use for try trade Snow-Owl out of her, so I tink I win her wid de cards. Den I was deal de skin game for Snow-Owl, un was hab heem broke —was geet all hees pony, all hees robe, was geet hees gun; but eet no use. Snow-Owl she not put de woman on de blanket. I tell heem, 'You put de woman on de blanket, by gar I put twenty pony un forty robe on de blanket.'

" No, he sais he weel not put de woman on de blanket. He nevair mind de robe un de pony. He go to de Absaroke un steal more pony, un he have de robe plenty by come snow.

"Well, he tak some young man un he go off to Absaroke to steal horse, un I seet roun' un watch dat woman. She watch me. Pretty soon camp was hunt de buffalo, un I was hunt Snow-Owl's woman. Every one was excite, un dey don' tak no 'count of me. I see de woman go up leetle coulie for stray horse, un I follar her. I sais: 'How do? You come be my woman. We run off to Meestar MacDonnail's tradehouse.'

"She sais she afraid. I tole her: 'Your buck no good; he got no robe, no pony; he go leave you to live on de

58

"HE SAIS HE WEEL NOT PUT DE WOMAN ON DE BLANKET"

camp. I am reech. Come wid me.'
And den I walk up un steek my knife
eento de ribs of de old camp pony
what she was ride. He was go hough!
hough! un was drop down. She was
say she weel go wid me, un I was tie
her hand un feet, all same cowboy she
rope de steer down, un I was leave her
dair on de grass. I was ride out een de
plain for geet my horse · ban', un was
tell my moccasin-boy I was wan' heem
go do dees ting, go do dat ting—I was
forget now.

"Well, den back I go wid de horse-
ban' to de woman, un was put her on
good strong pony, but I was tak off
hees lariat and was tie her feet undar
hees belly. I tink maybeso she skin
out. Den we mak trail for Meestar
MacDonnail, un eet was geet night. I
was ask her eef she be my squaw. She
sais she will be my squaw; but by gar

she was my squaw, anyhow, eef I not
tak off de rawhide." Sundown here
gave himself up to a little merriment,
which called crocodiles and hyenas to
my mind.

"I was tell you not for doubt I mak
dat horse-ban' burn de air dat night. I
knew eef dose Enjun peek up dat trail,
dey run me to a stan'-steel. Eet was
two day to Meestar MacDonnail, un I
got dair 'bout dark, un Meestar Mac-
Donnail she sais, 'When dose Enjun
was come een?' I sais, 'Dey come
pretty queek, I guess.'

"I was glad for geet een dat log
fence. My pony she could go no more.
Well, I was res' up, un maybeso eet
four day when up come de 'vance-guard
of dose Enjun, un dey was mad as wolf.
Deedn't have nothin' on but de moccasin un de red paint. Dey was crazy.
Meestar MacDonnail he not let 'em een

de log fence. Den he was say, 'What een hell de matter, Leflare?' I sais, 'Guess dey los' someting.'

"Meestar MacDonnail was geet up on de beeg gate, un was say, 'What you Enjun want?' Dey was say, 'Leflare; he stole chief's wife.' Dey was want heem for geeve me up. Den Meestar MacDonnail he got crazy, un he dam me terreble. He sais I was no beesness steal woman un come to hees house; but I was tol' heem I have no oddar plass for go but hees house. He sais, 'Why you tak woman, anyhow?' I was shrug my shouldair.

"Dose Enjun dey was set roun' on dair ham-bone un watch dat plass, un den pretty soon was come de village— dog, baby, dry meat—whole outfeet. Well, Leflare he was up in a tree, for dey was mak camp all roun' dat log fence. Meestar MacDonnail he was

geet on de gate, de Enjun dey was set
on de grass, un dey was talk a heap—
dey was talk steady for two day. De
Enjun was have me or dey was burn de
pos'. Meestar MacDonnail sais he was
geeve up de woman. De Enjun was
say, dam de woman—was want me. I
was say I was not geeve up de woman.
Dat was fine woman, un I was say eef
dey geet dat woman, dey mus' geet Le-
fiare firs'.

"All night dar was more talk, un de
Enjun dey was yell. Meestar MacDonnail was want me for mak run een de
night-time, but I was not tink I geet
troo. 'Well, den,' he sais, 'you geeve
yourself to dose Enjun.' I was laugh
at heem, un cock my breech-loadair, un
say, 'You cannot mak me.'

" De Enjun dey was shoot dar gun at
de log fence, un de white man he was
shoot een de air. Eet was war.

62

" All right. Pretty soon dey was mak de peace sign, un was talk some more. Snow-Owl had come.

" Den I got on de gate un I yell at dem. I was call dem all de dog, all de woman een de worl'. I was say Snow-Owl he dam ole sage - hen. He lose hees robe, hees pony, hees woman, un I leek heem een de bargain eef he not run lak deer when he hear my voice. Den I was yell, bah !" which Sundown did, putting all the prairie - dogs into their holes for our day's march.

" Den dey was talk.

" Well, I sais, eef Snow - Owl he any good, let us fight for de woman. Let dose Enjun sen' two beeg chief eento de log fence, un I weel go out eento de plain un fight Snow-Owl for de woman. Eef I leek, dose Enjun was have go 'way ; un eef dar was any one strike me but Snow-Owl, de two chief mus' die.

Meestar MacDonnail he say de two
chief mus' die. De Enjun was talk
heap. Was say 'fraid of my gun. I
was say eef I not tak my gun, den
Snow-Owl mus' not tak hees bow-arrow.
Den dey send de two chief eento de log
house. We was fight wid de lance un
de skin-knife.

"Eet was noon, un was hot. I was
sharp my knife, was tie up my bes'
pony tail, un was tak off my clothes,
but was wear my hat for keep de sun
out of my eye. Den I was geet on my
pony un go out troo de gate. I was yell,
'Come on, Snow-Owl; I teach you new
game ;' un I was laugh at dem.

"Dose Enjun weare not to come
within rifle-shot of de pos', or de chief
mus' die.

"All right. Out come Snow-Owl.
He was pretty man—pretty good man,
I guess. Oh, eet was long time 'go. I

tink he was brav' man, but he was tink too much of dat woman. He was on pinto pony, un was have not a ting on heem but de breech - clout un de bull-hide shiel'. Den we leek our pony, un we went for fight. I dun'no' jes what eet all weare;" and Sundown began to undo his shirt, hauling it back to show me a big livid scar through the right breast, high up by the shoulder.

" De pony go pat, pat, pat, un lak de light in de mornin' she trabel 'cross de plain we come togaddar. Hees beeg buffalo lance she go clean troo my shouldar, un br'ak off de blade, un trow me off my pony. Snow - Owl she stop hees pony chuck, chunck, chinck, un was come roun' for run me down. I peeked up a stone un trow eet at heem. You bet my medicine she good; eet heet heem een de back of de head.

"Snow - Owl she go wobble, wobble,

E   65

un she slide off de pony slow lak, un I was run up for heem. When I was geet dair he was geet on hees feet, un we was go at eet wid de knife. Snow-Owl was bes' man wid de lance, but I was bes' man wid de knife, un hees head was not come back to heem from de stone, for I keel him, un I took hees hair; all de time de lance she steek out of my shouldar. I was go to de trade-pos', un dose Enjun was yell terreble; but Meestar MacDonnail she was geet on de gate un say dey mus' go 'way or de chief mus' die.

"Nex' morning dey was all go 'way; un Leflare he go 'way too. Meestar MacDonnail he did not tink I was buy all my squaw. Sacré!

"Oh, de squaw — well, I sol her for one hundred dollar to white man on de Yellowstone. 'Twas t'ree year aftair dat fight;" and Sundown made a dé-

"HEES BEEG BUFFALO-LANCE SHE GO CLEAN TROO MY SHOULDAR"

tour into the brushy bottom to head back the kitchen-mare, while I rode along, musing.

This rough plains wanderer is an old man now, and he may have forgotten his tender feelings of long ago. He had never examined himself for anything but wounds of the flesh, and nature had laid rough roads in his path, but still he sold the squaw for whom he had been willing to give his life. How can I reconcile this romance to its positively fatal termination?

Back came Sundown presently, and spurring up the cut-bank, he sang out, "You tink I always buy my squaw, hey?—what you tink 'bout eet now?"

Oh, you old land-loper, I do not know what to think about you, was what came into my head; but I said, "Sundown, you are a raw dog," and we both laughed.

So over the long day's ride we bobbed along together, with no more romance than hungry men are apt to feel before the evening meal. We toiled up the hills, driving the pack-horses, while the disappearing sun made the red sand-rocks glitter with light on our left, and about us the air and the grass were cold. Presently we made camp in the canyon, and what with laying our bedding, cooking our supper, and smoking, the darkness had come. Our companions had turned into their blankets, leaving Sundown and me gazing into the fire. The dance of the flames was all that occupied my mind until Sundown said, " I want for go Buford dees wintair."

" Why don't you go ?" I chipped in.

" Oh—leetle baby—so long," and he showed me by spreading his hands about eighteen inches.

" Your baby, Sundown ?"

68

"Yees — my little baby," he replied, meditatively.

"Why can't you go to Buford?" I hazarded.

"Leetle baby she no stan' de trip. Eet varrie late een de fall — maybeso snow—leetle baby she no stan' dat."

"Why don't you go by railroad?" I pressed; but, bless me, I knew that was a foolish question, since Sundown Leflare did not belong to the railroad period, and could not even contemplate going anywhere that way.

"I got de wagon un de pony, but de baby she too leetle. Maybeso I go nex' year eef baby she all right. I got white woman up at agency for tak care of de baby, un eet cos' me t'ree dollar a week. You s'pose I put dat baby een a dam Enjun tepee?" And his voice rose truculently.

As I had not supposed anything concerning it, I was embarrassed somewhat, and said, " Of course not — but where was the mother of the child ?"

" Oh, her mudder—well, she was no Enjun. Don' know where she ees now. When de leetle baby was born, her mudder was run off on de dam railroad ;" and we turned in for the night.

My romance had arrived.

SUNDOWN LEFLARE'S MONEY

SUNDOWN LEFLARE'S MONEY

SITTING together comfortably on the front porch of the house of the man who ran the flouring-mill at the agency, Sundown and I felt clean, and we both had on fresh clothes. He had purchased at the trader's a cotton shirt with green stripes, which would hold the entire attention of any onlooker. We were inclined to more gayety than the smoke of the mountain camp-fire superinduced, and became more important and material when the repression of the great mountains was removed.

"Well, Sundown, how are you feeling?" I opened.

"Feelin' pretty reech dese day," he observed, with a smile.

"Have you paid the kid's board yet?"

"Ah, by gar, I was pay dose board-money 'fore I was geet off dat pony. How you s'pose I know what weel come when I was heet de agency? Firs' fellar she wiggle de pas'eboard maybeso Sundown go broke. Well, I was buy de shirt un de tobac. Good shirt, deese, hey? Well, den, I don' care."

"Of course you don't, my dear Mr. Leflare. Having money is a great damage to you," I continued.

"Yes, dat ees right. Money she no gran' good ting for Enjun man lak for white folk. Enjun she keep de money een hees han' 'bout long she keep de snow een hees han', but I was tell you eet was all he was geet dese day. Pony she not bring much. Enjun he can't mak de wagon 'less he 'ave de price.

De dry meat, de skin, un de pony, she
was what Enjun want; but he was geet
leetle now. Use for 'ave eet long time
'go; now not'ing but money! Dam!

"Back yondair, een what year you
call '80 — all same time de white man
was hang de oddar white man so fas'—
she geet be bad. De buffalo man she
was come plenty wid de beeg wagon,
was all shoot up de buffalo, was tak all
de robe. Den de man come up wid de
cow, un de soldier he was stop chasse
de Enjun. De Enjun she was set roun'
de log pos', un was not wan' be chasse
some more—eet was do no good. Den
come de railroad; aftar dat bad, all
bad. Was see peop' lak you. Dey was
'ave de money, un was all time scout
roun' un buy de cow. De man what
was sell de cow she buy de cow some
more; dey all done do not'ing but set
roun' un buy de cow. I could not geet

de buffalo, un could no more geet de
money for be soldier scout. Well, I
was not understan' — I was not know
what do. We was keel de cow once—
maybeso I tell you 'bout dat some time.
De cowboy she say we mus' not keel
de cow. We say, 'You keel our buffalo, now we mus' keel your cow.' He
sais soldiers dey geet aftar us, un we
don' know what do.

" I was say to Dakase un Hoopshuis:
' You mak de horse - ban' wid me. We
go on de Yellowstone un sell de cowboy de pony—mak great deal of money,' " continued Sundown.

In hopes of development, I asked
where he got all the ponies.

"Ah, nevar you min' dat. We was
geet dem pony where dey was cheap."
And I knew, from his cynicism, that it
was an ancient form of his misbehavior.
" So Dakase un me un Hoopshuis was

tak de horse-ban' to Yellowstone Reever, un was hole eet by Meestar John
Smeeth log house back een de foot-
heel. Meestar John Smeeth he was
sell de rum un deal de card in de log
house. De cowboy she stop roun'
Meestar John Smeeth log house, un de
cowboy was raise hell. Dees rum she
varrie bad medicin' for Enjun, all right;
un she varrie bad for cowboy, all same.
Cowboy he geet drunk, wan' all time
for burn hees seex-shootair. Bad plass
for Enjun when de cowboy she hise een
de rum.

"Well, 'long come de cow outfeet,
un Dakase un de oddar Enjun she was
pull out een de foot-heel, but I was stop
roun' for notice Meestar John Smeeth
sell de horse-ban' to de cowboy. Meestar John Smeeth she not be varrie bes'
man I evair was see. We all time look
at Meestar John Smeeth varrie sharp.

I was say to Meestar Smeeth, 'You sell de pony to de cowboy, un eef you geet 'nough money, you 'ave one horse when you was sell ten horse'; un I sais to heem : 'I tink you not ride varrie far on de beeg road eef you beat roun' much when you do beesness with us Enjun. I weel talk de Anglais to dose cowboy, un I weel find you out, Meestar John Smeeth.'

"'Long come de cowboy, un Meestar Smeeth she was try sell de pony; but de cowboy she weel not buy de pony, 'cause she say de bran'-iron not b'long Meestar John Smeeth. He sais, no, not b'long heem, b'long friend of hees.

" Dose cowboy dey laugh varric loud, un dey sais, 'Guess, Meestar Smeeth, you see your frien' troo de smoke.'

"Cowboys dey go 'way. Meestar Smeeth he sais, ' I mak dat bran' b'long me,' so Dakase un Hoopshuis un me,

un Meestar John Smeeth, we was work
t'ree day een de corral, un we was mak
dat bran' b'long Meestar John Smeeth.
All time dar weare a leetle white man
what was hang roun' de log house un
shuffle de card. He know how shuffle
dose card, I tell you. He was all time
fool wid de card. He wear de store
clothes, un he was not help us bran' de
horse - ban', 'cause he sais, ' Dam de
pony!'

" We wait roun', wait roun'. Oh, we
was eat Meestar Smeeth bacon, un we
was not strain ourself for de time. Meestar Smeeth he was fry de bacon un mak
de bread, un he geet varrie much hope
for noddar cow outfeet.

" T'ree men weare come 'long de
beeg stage-road. Dey sais dar name ees
Long-Horn. Well, I know what white
man she call de Long-Horn now, un I
'ave know since what he call de Short-

Horn. I tink ect good deal lak Enjun
call de Big-Robe; I tink ect good deal
lak John Smeeth. Dar ain't much
Long - Horn nowday, un dar ain't so
much John Smeeth as dar use be.

"All right, dey was buy de horse-
ban', un was pay de money right dar.
Dey was drive de pony on de beeg
stage-road. Meestar John Smeeth she
give us de money, un sais we weel play
de pokair a leetle. Dat was good beesness, so we was all set down een de
log house un play de pokair. Maybeso
we play one whole day. All right, dey
was geet every dam cent we got ; all de
money what was b'long Dakase un me
un Hoopshuis, un we was loss our pony
un our money.

"Dekase un Hoopshuis dey geet on
dar pony un go 'way, but I was stay at
de log house, for I was see dat de leetle
man she was deal us de skin game, but

I was not see how he was do de ting.
I was varrie much wan' for know how
he do ect, un was tell heem I was not
care eef he 'ave all my money, jus' so
he show me how he deal dat skin game.
I tell heem dat maybeso I keel heem
eef he not show me. Well, den he was
show me. He was rub my right thumb
wid de powder-stone, un de skin she
geet varrie sof'. Den he was show me
how feel de prick een de card, un he
was show me how feel de short end of
de card — dose cards was 'ave de one
end file' off. He was geeve me deck of
dose short card, un I was set een front
of dat log house, un look up at de cloud,
un feel dose prick un dose short card—
I was feel two day steady.

"Me un de store-clothes man we was
set een front of de log house, maybeso eet t'ree day, when up de road
come de t'ree Long-Horn white man

what had pay for de horse - ban'. Dey was run dar horse plenty.

" I was shut my eye pretty close, un I was tink pretty queck. I was tink great deal more queck dan I was tole you 'bout dees ting. I was say, ' Sundown, what mak dem t'ree white man run dem horse so fas'?' I was see why. I was say to myself, Dakase un Hoopshuis she 'ave steal dem pony. I geet up un sais, ' You store-clothes man, you run aftar me or you be keel' 'bout one minute'; un I was go roun' de corner of dat log house un geet een de cottonwoods; den we was mak de san' fly 'bout one mile. Pretty queck I was hear shootin', den I was hear not'ing. We was geet on a point of de rock, un we was see de white man : she look at our moccasin track. Dey was go back to log house, un go 'way up de stage-trail.

" I sais den : ' Store-clothes, Meestar John Smeeth ees all fix up for burn de candle ovair. Dem white mans have kill heem.'

" Den we go back, scout up de log house, un fin' Meestar John Smeeth— oh, all shoot up. He was fry de bacon when dose man weare pour de lead een heem.

" We was bury dees Smeeth, un I sais: ' Now, Meestar Store-clothes, you un I got for run lak hell. De cowboy he come pretty soon, un he come smokin'.'

" Store-clothes she sais cannot run on de horse.

" ' Well,' I sais, ' you cannot run on de foot, by gar ; de cowboy she 'ave your trail hot 'fore you tink.'

" I was geet down de pony from de foot-heel un was put de store-clothes man on one pony, un den I was herd dat pony all day un all night. He was groan terrible — oh, my, 'ow he was squawk, was dat leetle man! but I was leek de pony wid my rope, un de pony was run 'long pretty good wid de store-clothes man.

" He was say tak heem to railroad.

" ' No,' I sais; ' go tak you wid me. We play de skin game plass I know, un eef we win, den I tak you to railroad.'

" ' How far dees plass?' sais de leetle man.

" ' Ah—we geet dar eef de pony hole out.' Den we was 'ave de long talk. I was say I keel heem eef he lose. He was say de oddar fellar keel heem eef he win. ' Well,' I sais, ' I sure keel you, maybeso de oddar fellar dey won't —you 'ave de bes' chance wid me.'

" He sais who de oddar feller is?

" I tell heem dey part Enjun, part white man—dey was breeds lak me.

84

"I was know a breed outfeet on de breaks of de Mountain - Sheep Butte what was run de pony off un was sell heem. Dey was 'ave plenty money, un I tink we play de skin game on dem.

" When we was geet dar I was talk I fin' de store-clothes man out een de heel, un was bring heem in. He was not un-'erstan' de Enjun talk. He was not know a ting 'cept deal de card, but he was know dat all right.

" Dose breed weare set roun' de camp un deal de card un drink de rum for day or so. We was not play de card much, un de store - clothes man he was lose a leetle when he was tak de chance een. Pretty soon dar was 'bout t'ree man she 'ave de money what b'long whole outfeet, un de store-clothes man he sais, 'You geet pony all fix up for run off, un to-night we play de game.' I sais: 'You geet all de money by de

middle of de night-time, un don' you
mees cet — I keel you. I weel turn
every horse out de camp, un when I
mak de sign you follair me — queek.'
Eet was 'bout ten o'clock when we
was set down on de buffalo - robe un
play de pokair wid de t'ree man by de
fire. One man what was not play was
hole de spleet steek for give de light.

" Eet was not long 'fore I was lose all
de money what I was 'ave, what was
what de store - clothes man 'ad geeve
me. Den de leetle man she look at me,
un she varrie much scare. He weare
lak de snow ; guess he nevair see much
Enjun ; guess he not lak what he 'ave
see. I was geet up un was look at
de leetle man—was look varrie smart at
heem " — and here Sundown accompanied with a look which must have chilled
the soul of the frontier gambler.

" Den I was slide 'way een de dark.

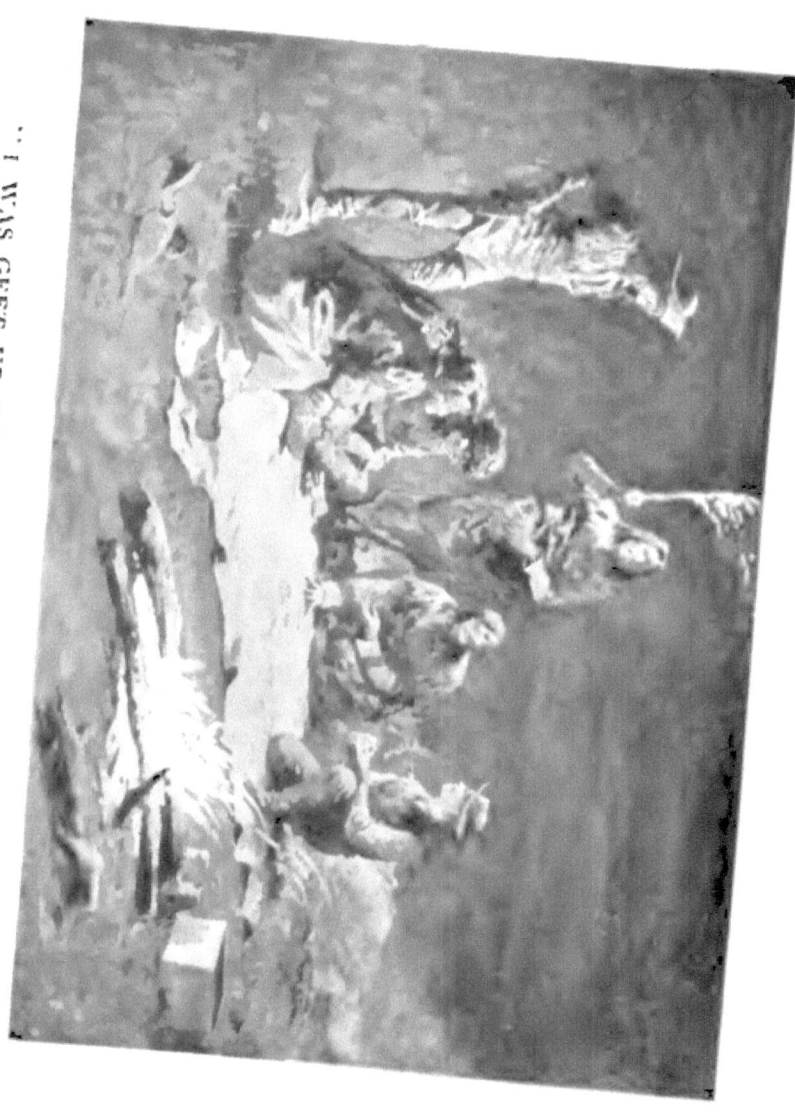

" I WAS GEET UP UN WAS LOOK AT' DE LEETLE MAN "

I was scout up dat camp. Dey was
mos' all drunk, 'cept de t'ree man what
was play de card. Dey was varrie mad,
but de leetle man was not know how
mad dose breeds was, 'cause de Enjun
when he varrie mad she don't look deff-
erent. Dey was lose dair money pretty
fas' to de leetle man.

"I was cut de rope of de pony all
roun' de camp, un dey was all go off
down de creek for de watair. Dey was
tie up long time. By gar, eef dar was
one man see me, eet be bad for de
store-clothes man, I tell you. Guess
dey keel heem. No one see me. I
was bring two pony up close to de
camp, quiet lak, un tie dem een de
bush. Den I was go to de fire. De
leetle man she look at me un she *cache*
all de money on de robe een hees pocket, un he tole me, 'You say I wan'
queet.' De breeds dey say he mus' not

queet. All right, he say, he play some
more. Den dey was play, un he was
deal, un dey was all 'ave de big han'ful,
un bet all dair money. I was know de
leetle man he sure win, un I was tak
out my seex-shootair.

" Den dese breed she got varrie much
excite. Oh, dey weare wild, un dey
weare show down dair han' on de robe.
De leetle man he was win all right. He
sais he sorry—he not wan' win all dair
money.

" I sais, ' You store-clothes man, you
put de money een your pocket; you
'ave win all right.' One man he sais he
'ave not win all right, un he mus' geeve
de money back. I was heet dees man
een de head wid my gun, un he was
fall down. Den dey was all jump up,
un de fellar what was hole de spleet
steek she drop de spleet steek. I was
jump to de leetle man un say, ' Come.'

"We run queck to dose bush, geet on de pony, un we geet out. Eet was so leetle time dat dese breed dey not *sabe*, un I don' know what dey do den. I herd dat store - clothes man on de pony, un he sais, ' Now you tak me to de railroad.'

" I sais: ' Yes, now I tak you to de railroad. Guess you tink dat pretty hot pokair game ?'

" He sais, eef he only geet to dat railroad ;" and Sundown laughed long and heartily.

" Guess dem breed fellars dey 'ave de long time for fin' dose pony. Eet was no use for me try herd dat leetle man fas' 'nough eef dose Enjun geet dose pony queck ; but dey deed not, so I was geet to Glendive, what was de end of de railroad. Dat store-clothes man he was great deal more teekle dan Meestar B—— when he geet dat bull elk oddar day. He was jump up un down; he was yell; he was tank me; he was buy great deal of rum. We was have varric good time.

"Den we was play de pokair some more—was play wid de white man. De leetle man was deal de card, un I was all time win. Was win all de white man was 'ave, un was geet a papier from one man what was what you call de mortgage for de leevery-stable. 'All right,' sais de lectle man, 'you put up your money—I put up my money un de papier—we tak de leevery-stable. Sundown,' he sais, 'we' go eento beesness—hey?'

"So we was go eento beesness—een de beesness of de leevery-stable. I was varrie great man.

"Dat was Saturday, un Sunday I was go out to see de pries', what was tole me to come. Aftair I was see de pries'

" HE WAS LAUGH AT ME FROM BETWEEN DE WHEEL."

un was fix up, I come back eento de village, un was go to de leevery-stable. Dey was say I not own de leevery-stable. 'You go see your pardner,' dey sais; un I geet on my pony for fin' leetle man what was my pardner. I look all roun'. De people was say he go off on de railroad. I was run dat pony for de dam railroad.

"When I was geet dar de train, what was de freight, she weare pull out. I was see de leetle store-clothes man—my pardner—she was stan' beside de train, un he was see me.

"I ride up, but he was jump on un-dair de car — what you call — de car-wheel axe, un he was laugh at me from between de wheel. He was yell, 'Sun-down, I blow cen de leevery-stable las' night.'

"'I weel blow you een,' I sais, un I fire de seex-shootair at heem, but I was unable to heet heem. De train was run fas'; my pony was not run so fas'—I could not catch heem. He was ride on de brake bettair dan on de pony;" and Sundown Leflare looked sad, for had not most of his real troubles come of railway trains?

"Well, Leflare," I said, as I thought of this meteoric financial tour, "nothing came of all that enterprise, did it?"

"No—no—not'ing came of dat."

SUNDOWN'S HIGHER SELF

SUNDOWN'S HIGHER SELF

I SAT in the growing dusk of my room at the agency, before a fire, and was somewhat lonesome. My stay was about concluded, and I dreaded the long ride home on the railroad—an institution which I wish from the bottom of my heart had never been invented.

The front door opened quietly, and shut. The grating or sand-paper sound of moccasined feet came down the hall, my door opened, and Sundown Leflare stole in.

" Maybeso you wan' some coal on dees fire — hey ?" he observed, looking in at the top of the stove.

"No, thank you — sit down," I replied, which he did, performing forthwith the instinctive act of making a cigarette.

"Sundown, I am going home to-morrow."

"Where you was go home?" came the guttural response.

"Back East."

"Ah, yees. I come back Eas' myself —I was born back Eas'. I was come out here long, long time 'go, when I was boy."

"And what part of the East did you come from?"

"Well—Pembina Reever—I was born een dat plass, un I was geet be good chunk of boy een dat plass—un, by gar, I wish I geet be dead man een dat plass. Maybeso I weel."

"You think you will go back some day?" I ventured.

"Oh, yees—I tink eet weel all come out dat way. Some day dat leetle baby he geet ole for mak de travel, un I go slow back dat plass. I mak dat baby grow up where dar ees de white woman un de pries'. I mak heem 'ave de farm, un not go run roun' deese heel on de dam pony." Sundown threw away his cigarette, and leaned forward on his hands.

"You are a Roman Catholic?" I asked.

"Yees, I am Roman Catholic. Dose pries' ees de only peop' what care de one dam 'bout de poor half-breed Enjun. You good man, but you not so good man lak de pries'. You go run roun' wid de soldier, go paint up deese Enjun, un den go back Eas'; maybeso nevair see you 'gain. Pries' he stay where we stay, un he not all de while wan' hear how I raise de hell ober de country. He keep say, 'You be good man, Sundown'; un, by gar, he keep tell me how for be good man.

"I be pretty good man now; maybe-so eet 'cause I too ole for be bad man;" and Sundown's cynicism had asserted itself, whereat we laughed.

It occurred to me that time had fought for the priest and against the medicine-man in these parts, and I so inquired.

"Yees, dey spleet even nowday. Pries' he bes' man for half-breed; but he be white man, un course he not know great many ting what dose Enjun know."

"Why, doesn't he know as much as the medicine-man?" came my infant-like question.

"Oh, well, pries' he good peop'; all time he varrie good for poor Sundown; but I keep tell you he ees white man. All time wan' tak care of me when I die. Well, all right, dees Enjun medicine-man she tak care of me when I was leeve sometime. You s'pose I wan' die all time? No; I wan' leeve; un I got de medicine ober een my tepee—varric good medicine. Eet tak me troo good many plass where I not geet troo may-beso."

" What is your medicine, Sundown?"

" Ah, you nevair min' what my medi-cine ees. You white man; what you know 'bout medicine? I see you 'fraid dat fores' fire out dair een dose moun-tain. You ask de question how dose canyon run. Well, you not be so 'fraid you 'ave de medicine. De medicine she tak care dose fire.

" White man she leeve een de house; she walk een de road; she nevair go half-mile out of hees one plass; un I guess all de medicine he care 'bout he geet een hees pocket.

" I see deese soldier stan' up, geet

keel, geet freeze all up ; don' 'pear care
much. He die pretty easy, un de pries'
he all time talk 'bout die, un dey don't
care much 'bout leeve. All time deese
die : eet mak me seeck. Enjun she wan'
leeve, un, by gar, she look out pretty
sharp 'bout eet too.

" Maybeso white man she don' need
medicine. White man she don' 'pear
know enough see speeret. Humph!
white man can't see wagon-track on de
grass ; don' know how he see wagon-
track on de cloud. Enjun he go all
ober de snow ; he lie een de dark ; he
leeve wid de win', de tunder—well, he
leeve all time out on de grass — night-
time—daytime—all de time."

" Yes, yes — certainly, Sundown. It
is all very strange to me, but how can
you prove to me that good comes to you
which is due to your medicine alone ?"

" Ah-h — my medicine — when weare

she evair do me any good? Ah-h, firs'
time I evair geet my medicine she save
my life—what? She do me great deal
good, I tell you. Eef dose pries' be
dair, she tell me, 'You geet ready for
die'; but I no wan' die.

"Well, fellar name Wauchihong un
me was trap de bevair over by de Souris Reever, un we weare not geet to dat
reever one night, un weare lay down for
go sleep. We weare not know where we
weare. We weare wak up een de middle of dat night, un de plain she all
great beeg grass fire. De win' she
weare blow hard, un de fire she come
'whew-o-o-o!' We say, where we run?
My medicine she tell me run off lef'
han', un Wauchihong hees medicine tell
heem you run off right-han' way. I
weare say my medicine she good; he
weare say hees medicine varrie ole—
have done de great ting—weare nevair

fail. We follow our medicine, un so
we weare part. I run varrie fas', un
leetle while I fall een de Souris Reever,
un den I know dose fire she not geet
Leflare. My medicine was good.

"Nex' day I fin' Wauchihong dead.
All burn — all black. He was burn up
een dose fire what catch heem on de
plain. De win' she drove de fire so fas'
he could do not'ing, un hees medicine
she lie to heem.

"You s'pose de pries' he tole me
wheech way for run dat night? No;
she tell me behave myself, un geet
ready for die right dair? Now what
you tink?"

Revelations and truths of this sort
were overpowering, and no desire to
change a man of Sundown's age and
rarity came to my mind; but in hopes
I said, "Did it ever so happen that
your medicine failed you?"

"My medicine she always good, but medicine ees not so good one time as nodder time. Do you s'pose I geet dat soldier order to Buford eef my medicine bad? But de medicine she was not ac' varrie well dat time.

"Deed you evair lie down alone een de bottom of de Black Canyon for pass de night? I s'pose you tink dair not'ing but bear een dat canyon ; but I 'ave 'ear dem speerets dance troo dat canyon, un I 'ave see dem shoot troo dem pine-tree when I was set on de rim-rock. Deed you evair see de top of dose reever een de moonlight? What you know 'bout what ees een dat reever? White man he don' know so much he tink he know. Guess de speeret don' come een de board house, but she howl roun' de tepee een de wintair night. Enjun see de speerets dance un talk plenty een de lodge fire ; white man he see not'ing but de coffee boil.

"White men mak de wagon, un de seelver dollar, un de dam railroad, un he tink dat ees all dair ees een de country;" and Sundown left off with a guttural "humph," which was the midship shot of disaster for me.

"But you don't tell the priest about this medicine?"

"No — what ees de use for tell de pries'?—he ees white man."

I asked Sundown what was the greatest medicine he ever knew, and he did not answer until, fired by my doubts, he continued, slowly, " My medicine ees de great medicine."

A critic must be without fear, since he can never fully comprehend the intent of other minds, so I saw that fortune must favor my investigations, for I knew not how to proceed; but knowing that action is life, I walked quickly to my gripsack and took out my silver pocket - flask, saying : " You know, Sundown, very well, that it is dead against the rule to give a redskin a drink on a United States agency, but I am going to give you one if you will promise me not to go out and talk about it in this collection of huts. Are you with me ?"

" Long-Spur—we pretty good frien' —hey ? I weel not say a ting."

Then the conventionalities were gone through with, and they are doubtless familiar to many of my readers.

" Now I tole you dees ting — what was de great medicine—but I don' wan' you for go out here een de village un talk no more dan I talk—are you me ?"

" I am you," and we forgathered.

" Now le's see ; I weel tole you 'bout de bigges' medicine," and he made a cigarette.

" You aire young man—I guess may-

beso you not born when I was be medicine-man ; but eet was bad medicine for
Absaroke, un you mus' not say a ting
'bout dees to dem. I am good frien'
here now, but een dose day I was good
frien' of de Piegan, un dey wan' come
down here to de Absaroke un steal de
pony. De party was geet ready — eet
was ten men, un we come on de foot.
We come 'long slow troo de mountain
un was hunt for de grub. Aftair long
time we was fin' de beeg Crow camp—
we was see eet from de top of de Pryor
Mountain. Den we go 'way back up
head of de canyon, 'way een dat plass
where de timber she varrie tick, un we
buil' de leetle log fort, 'bout as beeg as
t'ree step 'cross de meddle. We was
wan' one plass for keep de dry meat;
we weare not wan' any one for see our
fire ; un we weare put up de beeg fight
dair eef de Absaroke she roun' us up.

"WE COME 'LONG SLOW TROO DE MOUNTAIN"

"Een dose day de Enjun he not come een de mountain varrie much—dey was hunt de buffalo on de flat, but maybeso she come een de mountain, un we watch out varrie sharp. Every night, jus' sundown, we go out — each man by hees self, un we watch dat beeg camp un de horse ban's. Eet was 'way out on de plain great many mile. White man lak you he see not'ing, but de Enjun he mak out de tepee un de pony. I was always see much bettair dan de oddar Enjun — varrie much bettair — un when we come back to de log fort for smoke de pipe, I was tole dose Enjun jus' how de country lay, un where de bes' plass for catch dem pony."

I think one who has ever looked at the Western landscape from a mountain-top will understand what Sundown intended by this extensive view. If one has never seen it, words will hardly tell him how it stretches away, red, yellow, blue, in a prismatic way, shaded by cloud forms and ending among them —a sort of topograghical map. I can think of nothing else, except that it is an unreal thing to look at.

"Well, for begeen wid, one man she always go alone; nex' night noddair man go. Firs' man she 'ave de bes' chance, un eet geet varrie bad for las' man, 'cause dose Enjun dey catch on to de game un watch un go roun' for cut de trail. But de Enjun horse-t'ief he mak de trail lak de snake — eet varrie hard for peek up.

"I was 'ave de idea I geet de medicine-man, un I tole dem dey don' know not'ing 'cause dey cannot see, un I tole dem I see everyting; see right troo de cloud. I say each dose Enjun now you do jus' what I tole you, den you fin' de pony.

"So de firs' man he was start off een de afternoon, un we see heem no more. When de man was geet de horse, un maybeso de scalp, he skin out for de Piegan camp.

"Nex' night noddair man she go start off late een de afternoon, un I go wid heem, un I sais, 'You stay here, pull your robe ovair your head, un I go een de brush un mak de medicine for tell where ees good plass for heem to go.' When I was mak de medicine I come back, un we set dair on de mountain, un I tell heem where he go 'way out dair on de plain. I sais: 'You go down dees canyon un follow de creek down, un twenty-five mile out dair you fin' de horse ban'. You can sleep one night een de plass where I was point heem out—den you geet de pony. Eef you not fin' eet so, I am not medicine-man.'

"So dees man was go. One man she go every night, un I was set een de log fort all 'lone las' night. I was say eef deese Enjun she do what I tole heem, I be beeg great medicine-man dees time. Den I geet varrie much scare, for I was las' man, un dose Absaroke dey sure begin see our trail, un I put out de fire een de log fort, un I go off down de mountain for geet 'way from de trail what deese Enjun she mak. I was wan' mak de fire on dees mountain, 'cause she jus' 'live wid dose grizzily bear. I varrie much 'fraid — I sleep een de tree dat night, un jus' come day I was go down de creek een de canyon. I was walk een de water un walk on de rocks. I was geet beeg ban' elk to run ovair my trail. I was walk 'long de rim-rock, un was geet pretty well down een de plain. I was sleep dat night een de old bear-cave, un I was see dees camp pretty

"I SAIS: 'YOU GO DOWN PEES CANYON'"

well. Eet was good plass, 'bout ten mile out een de uppair valley of de Beeg-Horn Reever, but I was 'ave be careful, for dose Enjun dey weare run all ovair de country hunt deese horse-t'ief tracks. Oh, I see dem varrie well. I see Enjun come up my canyon un pass by me so near I hear dem talk. I was scare.

"Jus' come dark I crawl up on de rim-rock, un eet was rain hard. Enjun she no lak de rain, so I sais: 'I go down now. I keep out een de heel, for I see varrie much bettair dan de Absaroke, un eef I tink dey see me I drop een de sage-bush.'" And here Sundown laughed, but I did not think such hide-and-seek was very funny.

"Eet geet varrie dark, un I walk up to dees camp, not more dan ten step from de tepee. I tak de dry meat off de pole un trow eet to dose dog for

mak dem keep still while I was hear de
Absaroke laugh un talk. De dog he
bark not so much at de Enjun as eef I
be de white man ; jus' same de white man
dog he bite de dam leg off de Enjun.

"I cut de rope two fine pony what
was tie up near de lodge, un I know
deese weare war-pony or de strong buffa-
lo-horse. I lead dem out of dose camp.
Eet was no use for try geet more as de
two pony, for I could not run dem een
de dark night. I feel dem all ovair for
see dey all right. I could not see much.
Den I ride off."

"You got home all right, I suppose?"

"Eef I not geet home all right, by
gar, I nevair geet home 'tall. Dey
chasse me, I guess, but I 'ave de good
long start, un I leave varrie bad trail, I
tink. Man wid de led horse he can
leave blind trail more def'rent dan when
he drive de pony.

"When I geet to dat Piegan camp I was fin' all dose Enjun 'cept one: he was nevair come back. Un I sais my medicine she ees good; she see where no one can see. Dey all sais my medicine she varrie strong for steal de pony. I was know ting what no man she see. Dey was all fin' de camp jus' as I say so. I was geet be strong een dat camp, un dey all say I see bes' jus' at sundown, un dey always call me de sundown medicine."

I asked, "How did it happen that you could see so much better than the others; was it your medicine which made it possible?"

"No. I was fool dose Enjun. I was 'ave a new pair of de fiel'-glass what I was buy from a white man, un I was not let dose Enjun see dem—dat ees how."

"So, you old fraud, it was not your

medicine, but the field-glasses?" and I jeered him.

"Ah, dam white man, she nevair understan' de medicine. De medicine not 'ave anyting to do wid de fiel'-glass; but how you know what happen to me een dat canyon on dat black night? How you know dat? Eef eet not for my medicine, maybeso I not be here. I see dose speeret — dey was come all roun' me — but my medicine she strong, un dey not touch me."

"Have a drink, Sundown," I said, and we again forgathered. The wild man smacked his lips.

"I say, Sundown, I have always treated you well; I want you to tell me just what that medicine is like, over there in your tepee."

"Ah, dat medicine. Well, she ees leetle bagful of de bird claw, de wolf tooth, t'ree arrow - head, un two bullet what 'ave go troo my body."

" Is that all ?"

" Ah, you white man !"

THE END

THE ODD NUMBER SERIES

16mo, Cloth, Ornamental

HARPER & BROTHERS, PUBLISHERS

NEW YORK AND LONDON

☞ *Any of the above works will be sent by mail, postage prepaid, to any part of the United States, Canada, or Mexico, on receipt of the price.*

By S. R. CROCKETT

THE RED AXE. A Novel. Illustrated by FRANK RICHARDS.

Mr. Crockett can always be depended upon for a good story, and his many admirers will not be disappointed by the "The Red Axe," which is an uncommonly strong novel of adventure.—*Brooklyn Standard-Union.*

LOCHINVAR. A Novel. Illustrated by T. DE THULSTRUP.

Admirers of S. R. Crockett will find occasion for neither surprise nor disappointment in his new story, "Lochinvar." It is just what we might expect of him after the assurance his other writings have given of the stability of his capacity for fine romantic fiction. He gives every indication that he is in the plenitude of his powers and graces as a constructionist and narrator.—*Washington Times.*

THE GRAY MAN. A Novel. Illustrated by SEYMOUR LUCAS, R.A.

A strong book, . . . masterly in its portrayals of character and historic events.—*Boston Congregationalist.*

Post 8vo, Cloth, Ornamental, $1 50 per volume.

HARPER & BROTHERS, PUBLISHERS
NEW YORK AND LONDON

☞ Any of the above works will be sent by mail, postage prepaid, to any part of the United States, Canada, or Mexico, on receipt of the price.